KALPA TARU

KSHAMA

I dedicate this book to the Lords of Kaliyug, their devotees, and readers of this book.

Contents

BHANU
The bright one.
BHAVYA
The auspicious one.
PAAVANA
The purifier.
DHANADA
The bestower of wealth.
DHANUSHMAT
The archer.
TAMASA
One associated with Tamoguna.
PASHUNAMPATI
The lord of animals.
NILACHCHATRA
The one with a blue umbrella.
NIRAMAYA
The one who is free from diseases.
NINDYA
The blamable one.
DIVYADEHA
The one with a heavenly body.
KRURA
The cruel one.

CHAPTER FIVE

VAHAN'S OF LORD SHANI

SHANI DEV'S VEHICLES

CROW

Shani Dev's favorite color is black and crow is black. This is the reason Shani Dev chose crow as his vehicle. Crow is a sharp-witted bird. It indicates Pitru in Hindu mythology. It can adjust in every environment. Just like Shani Dev, the crow also indicates darkness, sadness, and death. Crow is very flexible and helps Shani Dev. Shani Dev removes the sadness and sufferings of his devotees when he comes sitting on a crow. Once Shani Dev and goddess Lakshmi had an argument about who is better. Lakshmi said that she is better as she bestows prosperity and happiness and Shani Dev said that he is better than her as he maintains justice. Shani said to Lakshmi that she can't differentiate between good and bad as she stays with bad people too. Lakshmi became angry and replied, "You are detrimental and no one wants to invite you. Everyone prays for your departure. You create a sense of terror". Then they both went to Brahma and asked him to conclude who is better. Brahma Dev didn't want to make any one of them angry and he asked them to go to Vishnu. Vishnu asked them to go to Lord Shiva. Shiva requested them to ask Narada Muni. After thinking, Narada muni said that Lakshmi looks good when she comes and Lord Shani looks good when he goes. From this day, their vehicles also became opponents as they wanted their masters to be the best and till today, the owl and the crow are enemies.

VULTURE

Vulture is also Shani Dev's vehicle. Vulture likes to feed on dead bodies. The urine of vultures can kill bacteria. The wings of a vulture are very powerful. The vulture maintains the natural cycle just like Shani Dev maintains the Karma. A vulture has a sharp eye and can take oxygen in any situation. The guilty will get the illness and death when Shani Dev uses this vehicle.

SWAN

Swan is a beautiful bird. It indicates peace, love, and beauty. Shani Dev always fortifies pure love. Shani Dev grants devotees peace when he rides on a swan.

PEACOCK

Shani Dev gives auspicious results when he comes riding on a peacock as luck favors the native and he can conquer any difficulty. Once Shani Dev was worshipping Krishna but Krishna didn't appear before him. So Shani Dev requests a peacock to live with him. Shani Dev sits on the backside of the peacock while it dances. Lord Krishna becomes happy with this and he appears before Shani Dev and requests him to use the peacock as his vehicle.

DOG

The dog is an honest animal. It can understand the language of spirits. It can see the air. It has a sharp-smelling power. According to a story, Shani Dev took the help of a dog to find out a devil, who was hiding, and from that day he rides on it. He always uses a dark black dog for riding.

DONKEY

One day a donkey named Bheema was waiting for its master. Shani Dev, observes that the master is not at all concerned about the donkey. Shani Dev pushed its master into a river. The donkey started screaming. He observed that the donkey is very much concerned about his master and the man is not worthy to keep this precious donkey. From that day, he keeps the donkey for himself. Lord Shani Dev gives problems when he enters a native's chart sitting on a donkey. The native will do the hard work but get fewer results.

LION

A lion is a powerful animal. When Shani Dev rides on a lion, he destroys the evils and this indicates victory.

BULL

Bull indicates power. Shani Dev rides with a sword to kill the enemies when he rides on a bull.

ELEPHANT

Elephants symbolize wisdom. Shani Dev, accepted the elephant as his vehicle when he became the king of Shani lok. Since then, Shani Dev has been known as Shani Maharaj. He rains riches when he rides on an elephant. Lakshmi told Shani dev that all royal kings have elephants so, Shani Dev also adopted the elephant as his vehicle.

CHAPTER SIX

WHY OFFER MUSTARD OIL TO SHANI DEV

As a child, Shani Dev was very errant. Hanuman was in charge of the Setu dam and one day, he was sitting on it and meditating. Shani Dev came there and teased Hanuman for sitting in the middle of the bridge. Hanuman politely replied that he is meditating and asked Shani Dev not to bother him. Shani Dev didn't listen and this is when Hanuman Ji trapped Shani Dev in his tail and tightened the grip. Hanuman Ji hit his tail on the bridge to break Shani Dev's pride. This caused wounds on Shani Dev's body. He prayed to Hanuman Ji to free him. Then Hanuman Ji gave him mustard oil to apply and said that his wounds will fade. From this day mustard oil is offered to Shani Dev. Shani Dev grants special blessings to devotees of Lord Hanuman.

CHAPTER SEVEN

LORD SHANI DEV AND CURSE OF HIS WIFE

Lord Shani has eight wives and he becomes happy if devotees chant their names on Saturdays. All his wives love and support him very much. Their names are as follows:

Dhamini, Dhwajini, Kanjali, Kalahpriya, Kantaki, Turangi, Mahishi and Aja.

His wife Dhamini is a Gandharva princess who is very beautiful, quick-witted, and an elegant dancer. One-day Dhamini got a desire to have a child from Shani Dev but Shani Dev was busy meditating. Dhamini made an effort to wake him up from meditation, but all her efforts went in vain and she became angry at Shani Dev. She cursed him that whoever Shani Dev will look upon will get bad luck. Later she regretted but her power could not be reversed. From that day, Shani Dev keeps his head down to avoid his devotees getting misfortune. Later the couple was blessed with a son and they named him Gulika. Blue Sapphire gemstone protects its wearer from the malefic sight of Lord Shani. This gemstone is named after his wife Neelima.

The Pandavas were exiled to Saturn's influence in their horoscope.

LORD SHANI AND LORD KRISHNA

Lord Shani didn't spare Lord Krishna too. Krishna was accused of robbing Syamantakamani, a precious jewel. People also mistook him for killing the king to steal the jewel. He had to face many insults and in the end, Shani Dev let him.

THREE DAUGHTER-IN-LAW OF A POOR FARMER AND LORD SHANI

Once a poor farmer had a wife, three sons, and three daughters-in-law. That day it was the youngest daughter-in-law's turn to look after the house. Lord Shani had appeared in the form of a Lepor and he had asked the lady to apply oil on his back and give him a bath as he had pain in his body. The lady felt pity for him and did the same and also provided him with some food. The leper blessed her that she will not have short of anything in life. Her in-laws became surprised to see mouth-watering and aromatic recipes in spite of their poverty. The next day the leper came again and the middle daughter-in-law was in charge of the house on that day. She got irritated by seeing the leper. Lord Shani Dev cursed the lady and there was no food on that day. On the third day, the first daughter-in-law was in charge of the household duties and Lord Shani cursed her too as she didn't care for him. On the last Saturday of that Shravan month, again the youngest daughter-in-law was in charge of the duties and the leper blessed her. Her in-laws also found pearls and diamonds in the leaf she served him food. They understood that it is the god who had come in disguise.

LORD SHANI AND NAMBIGAL

Nambigal, used to offer services to Lord Varadharaja Perumal and to a guru to Shri Ramanujar. He requested Lord Shani to reduce the period of Sade Sati as it may cause inconvenience in the service to god. Lord Shani reduced the span of his gaze to seven and a half hours. The next day, the golden bowl went missing from the temple and the officials there suspected Nambigal. Nambigal couldn't prove that he was innocent. By this time, seven and a half hours passed and the officials found the gold bowl. They apologized to Nambigal.

CHAPTER NINE

OTHER STORIES ABOUT SHANI DEV AND HIS MALEFIC SIGHTS

LORD SHANI AND RAVANA

Meghanad was the son of Ravana and Mandodari. Ravana wanted that his son's horoscope and the planetary positions should be flawless so that his son can become immortal. Ravana captured all the nine planets and tormented them. By seeing this Narada muni, challenged Lord Shani dev and he got provoked. Shani teased Ravana that he is a weakling which is why he has put all the planets facing downwards under his seat. Ravana became angry and he turned all the planets to face up. Lord Shani cast his eye on Ravana and created a yoga by which Ravana will be killed by Rama and Meghanad will have a short life span.

LORD SHANI AND DAKSHA

Shani Dev had gazed Daksha's horoscope. So he had lost his mind. He didn't grant permission to Sati to marry Shiva as he didn't have his standard of living. Sati had married

Lord Shiva against her father's will. Daksha had arranged a yajna and invited all gods except Shiva and Sati. Sati attended the Yagya without invitation in spite of Shiva warning her not to go. There she had to face insult by Daksha and she fell into the fire. Lord Shiva becomes furious and performed Tandava and cut Daksha's head. Later he attached a goat's head to Daksha and brought him back to life.

LORD SHANI AND VIKRAMADITYA

Once the navagrahas had a fight amongst themselves about who is the best. They went to Lord Indra. He didn't want to take sides and acted cleverly. He suggested they go to King Vikramaditya of Ujjain. King Vikramaditya was famous for justice. He arranged nine thrones. The first was made of gold and the other was made of other metals. The ninth was made of iron and it was of lower rank according to the king. He asked the nine planets to choose their throne. Lord Shani chose the ninth crown as he had a natural affinity toward iron, but he became angry when Vikramaditya declared him the lowest rank. He warned the king that his bad days have started from that day. King Vikramaditya lost his limbs and started doing hard work. After seven and a half years, Lord Shani returned him everything he had seized from him. The king asked his subjects to fast on Saturdays and worship Lord Shani to get relief from the sufferings they get from Saturn.

CHAPTER TEN

KNOW MORE ABOUT SHANI DEV

Lord Shani is the judge of our deeds. Lord Shani gives us rewards and punishments for our past sins and deeds. He is not a wrongdoer. It is all about our planetary positions. He helps us delete our past sins so that we can attain liberation. Kanchi Periyava guru also says the same. We need not fear Lord Shani.

We should seek a good guru for guidance. Worshipping gods like Ayappa, Ganesha, Dakshinamurthy, Kala Bairava, and Narasimha also can save us from the malefic effects of Saturn. Chanting Shani Gayatri mantra, Shani beej mantra – Om pram preem pra um sah Shanaischaraya Namaha, Shani kavach, Shani Chalisa, Dasharatha krutha Shani stotra, Aditya hridaya, Vishnu sahasranama, Lalita sahasranama, reading Nalacharita on Saturday or on Amavasya is beneficial. We can do ellu thiri in Shani temples. Thirunallar Shani temple, Agasteeswarar temple in Chennai, Kuchanur Shaneeshwara Bhagawan temple, Pongu Sani temple, Kailasnathar temple, Shani Singnapur, Shani devalayam - Mumbai, Titwala Shani temple, Shani Dham – Delhi where 21 feet tall Shani statue made of Ashtadhatu is there, Shanimahatma temple, Chikka madhure, Shani temple, Madhya Pradesh where you can take parikrama of Shani parvat to get rid of his malefic effects, Shani temple –Indore, Shani dev mandir-Kota-Rajasthan, Bannanje Sri Shani Kshetra, Yerdnur Shani temple, Mandapalli mandeswara Swamy temple-Andhra Pradesh, Shaneeshwara Kshetram-Kerala, Eramathur Shaneeshwra temple-Kerala are famous Shani temples and worshipping Lord Shani in these temples can reduce his malefic effects.

CHAPTER ELEVEN

METHODS OF PLEASING SHANI DEV

Saturn rules bone, nervous system, teeth and bones. Light a sesame oil lamp in the east and pray to Shani God. Don't keep his photo. Just pray in your mind. Offer water to the Peepal tree and light a lamp in front of it in the evening. Offer blue colour flowers or any other flowers to Lord Shani. Chant Shani mantras. Help the handicapped, needy, old, labourers and poor people. Donate them food, black cloth and money. Feed animals and birds. Feed black dogs and cows. Feed raisins to crows in the morning. When worshipping Lord Shani in the temple, don't stand directly in front of him. You should stand on the side and worship him. Don't look into his eyes. Look at his feet while offering the oil and black cloth to Lord Shani in the temple. Chanting the Mahamrityunjay mantra is very beneficial. Listening to Sunderkand and Hanuman Chalisa on Tuesday and Saturday is very beneficial. Worship goddess Katyayini. Remove clutter from your house. Wear a black horseshoe ring on the middle finger of your left hand on Saturday. Fasting on Saturdays will please Saturn. Don't buy iron goods, mustard oil, sesame and black things on Saturday. You can buy a broom on Saturday. Donate slippers to the poor or needy. Worship a black cow and circumambulate it to get rid of Sade Sati. Visiting Lord Venkateshwara's shrine at Tirupati is highly favourable. Worshipping Garuda and Sudarshana Chakra helps in protecting ourselves from the malefic effects of Saturn. Please your ancestors and do your duty. Quit non-vegetarian food and alcohol.

Include black pepper and salt in your diet. Wear black datura as a pendant or as an amulet. You can tie black datura in a black cloth and tie it on your left arm. Wear a blue sapphire and seven Mukhi rudraksha.

A favourable Shani will bestow you with a strong career, healthy life, prosperity, fame and leadership.

Lord Shani comes into a person's life three times. He gives a lot of worries when he comes in the early hood, in the middle age he gives financial problems and in the old age slow growth is seen and finally, Saturn relieves his clasp. You should worship Lord Saturn on Shani Amavasya.

During Sade Sati, Dhaiya, Panchama Shani, ashtama Shani, kantaka Shani, Shani mahadasha and antardasha Saturn casts his sight on the native. But again it all depends on Karma, whether Shani will punish you or reward you. If Saturn is favourable he will bless you. Shani is also a yogakaraka. He causes Shasha yoga in the horoscope.

LORD HANUMAN

Lord Hanuman is the Lord of Kaliyug as he is a Chiranjeevi and is present even today. It is difficult to recognize him in any form. He is a devotee of Rama. He comes to places where the glories of Rama and Sita are told.

Hanuman belongs to the ‘Kapi’ family. ‘Kapi’s had a face and tail like a monkey but a body like humans. They were very brave and bright. In many countries like Indonesia, India, Jakarta, and Thailand, they ruled like kings. Later, they vanished. The ’Hanuman Chalisa‘ is a forty hymn line which addresses Lord Hanuman. Tulsidas has authored it in the ’Awadhi‘ language. Tulsidas also wrote Rama Charita Manasa. If we feel any fear then we should chant ’Hanuman Chalisa'.

CHAPTER TWELVE

BIRTH OF LORD HANUMAN

Lord Hanuman is an incarnation of Lord Shiva. His mother is 'Anjani' an apsara. She served saint Agastya who was very short-tempered and he cursed for her a petty mistake to become a monkey at her next birth. After apologizing, Agastya showed mercy on her and said that Lord Shiva can grant her a boon if she worships him. Anjani meditated on Lord Shiva and he granted her a boon that he will come out of her womb in her next birth.

Anjani was born as a monkey after a few years. She married'Keshari'. The couple was not having children so Anjani meditated on Lord Shiva and 'Pawan Dev' used his force to carry the divine power of Shiva to Anjani's womb as a blessing. The baby born was named 'Hanuman'. Hanuman is also known as Pawan putra.

CHAPTER THIRTEEN

LITTLE BABY HANUMAN WAS HUNGRY

One day baby Hanuman was very hungry. He wanted to eat fruits but there were no fruits in his garden. He saw a red fruit in the sky. He flew high towards the sky and enlarged himself to eat the sun. The reality is that Lord Hanuman is hungry for knowledge as the sun represents knowledge. The whole world became dark. Indra became very angry and hit Hanuman with his thunderbolt. Hanuman fell to the ground. Lord Shiva and Pawan fathers of Hanuman became very angry with Indra. Shiva did Tandav and Pawan Dev stopped wind of air. Then other Devatas blessed baby Hanuman with their powers and pleased Shiva and Pawan Dev.

CHAPTER FOURTEEN

ROLE OF HANUMAN IN THE RAMAYANA

Hanuman was very naughty as a child and was not using his powers. Due to this, he was cursed by a saint to lose all his powers. Later the saint blessed him that when Hanuman is reminded of his powers by someone his powers will be regained.

Lord Hanuman, along with his companions had helped Lord Shri Ram to find Sita, when Ravana had kidnapped her. Lord Hanuman feared to cross the river to find Sita and Jamwant, a bear who was his father Kesari's friend, reminded him of his powers. Lord Hanuman leaped the 100 Yojana sea and found Sita crying in Ashokavatika. He showed Sri Rama's ring to her and consoled her. Later the soldier of Lanka set fire to his tail as he had destroyed their garden in search of fruits. Lord Hanuman burnt all the buildings of Lanka from his tail and crossed the sea by quenching the fire in the sea.

With the help of Neel and Nal who are sons of Vishwakarma the architect god, they all built a bridge and crossed the sea. There, in the war, Meghanath injured Sri Rama and Lakshmana with his snake loop. Lord Hanuman requested Garuda to help them and relieve them from the snake loop. Vaidya Raja Sushain then checked Lakshmana who was severely injured and asked Hanuman to get Sanjeevani Booti from the Himalayas. Lord Hanuman uprooted the whole mountain as he failed to recognize the herb. All praised Hanuman's bravery and because of him, Lakshman became alive.

Vibhishana brother of Ravana supported Rama and revealed many secrets about Ravana as he was against supporting the evil. Lakshmana killed Meghanath and Ravana attacked Rama. Ravana's head appeared again and again and it seemed impossible for Rama to kill Ravana. Then, Vibhishana revealed that his life is located in his navel and he can be killed by a special weapon that only he and his wife Mandodari knows. Mandodari was a religious woman and used to give alms to the poor and needy people. Lord Shiva and Lord Hanuman too, went to her and begged for alms. Mandodari understood that these two are not normal human beings and requested them to disclose their identity. Lord Hanuman addressed her as mother and begged for the weapon as alms. Mandodari understood that it is Lord Shiva's order and gave them the weapon as alms. In the war, Ravana died as Sri Ram hit him with this weapon in his navel. All this happened only because of Lord Hanuman's intelligence and courage.

After reaching Ayodhya, Sri Ram gifted everyone who helped him in the war. Lord Hanuman said that he does not need any gift and he just wants to be with Lord Sri Ram all the time. Because of his statement, a few people started doubting him, and then he ripped his chest and showed Sri Ram and Sita in his heart. Sri Rama blessed him with immortality but Lord Hanuman said that he only wants a position near Sri Ram's feet.

One day he saw Mata Sita applying sindoor in her hair partition and asked the reason for doing so. Sita replied that she applies it for Sri Ram's longevity. Listening to this Lord Hanuman applied Sindoor all over his body.

CHAPTER FIFTEEN

LORD HANUMAN AND LORD SHANI DEV

There is a belief that Lord Hanuman does not suffer from Shani Dev. Another belief is that all planets are under the tail of Lord Hanuman. There is a story, that Lord Hanuman had saved Lord Shani Dev and all the other nine planets from the hold of Ravana.

Ravana had imprisoned all the nine planets. Lord Hanuman who had come there in search of Sita had heard Lord Shani Dev crying for help and Lord Hanuman had freed him but as soon as Shani Dev set his eyes on him Lord Hanuman became a victim of his cruel gaze. Lord Hanuman doesn't have any family and his life is dedicated to Lord Rama so he was able to bear the trouble.

He fought with the demons and he lifted heavy mountains and rocks and Lord Shani was sitting on his head. Lord Shani was hurt and he started bleeding when Lord Hanuman crushed rocks with his head. Lord Shani moved to Lord Hanuman's shoulders. Now, Lord Hanuman carried a huge mountain and again Lord Shani suffered due to pain and requested Hanuman to set him free. " You are the one who is not affected by my gaze. I would like to give you a boon as you have saved me from the clutches of Ravana, so please ask whatever you want," said Shani Dev. Lord Hanuman asked Shani Dev not to trouble his devotees and Lord Shani promised that he will moderate his malefic effects on devotees of Lord Hanuman. Lord Shani asked for some oil as his pain was unbearable. Lord Hanuman gave him mustard oil and they both sat under a Peepal tree. Lord Hanuman massaged Lord Shani Dev with this oil and all his pain got relieved. People who worship Hanuman on Saturday are not affected by Lord Saturn's malefic gaze. We should not buy oil on Saturday but we should offer oil to Lord Hanuman and Lord Shani on Saturday. There is a spiritual relationship between Lord Hanuman and Lord Shani. Lord Shani is egoistic and Lord Hanuman is humble. So we should be humble during Saturn periods and should develop a sense of service.

CHAPTER SIXTEEN

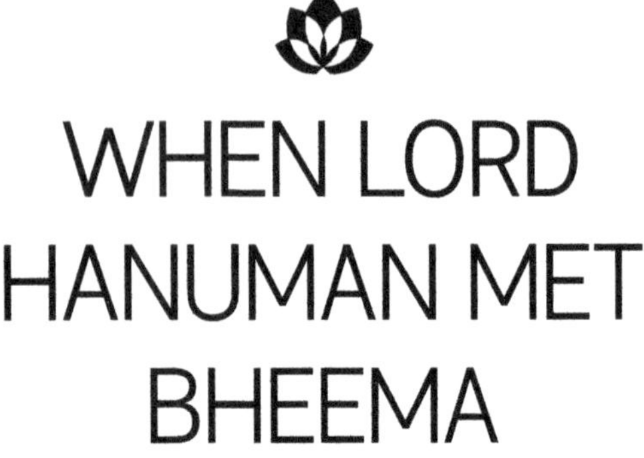

WHEN LORD HANUMAN MET BHEEMA

One day Draupadi had brought a fragrant flower from the northeast direction. She asked Bheema to get more such flowers. Bheema entered a forest 'Kadlivan'. Lord Hanuman was lying there disguised as an old monkey. Bheema asked the monkey to go to a side and sleep there. Hanuman replied that he should not have wakened him up as he is old and he requested him to move his tail aside and go. Bheema became angry and tried to set aside his tail, but he couldn't move it. He got surprised and his pride got crushed. Hanuman started smiling and Bheema asked for his forgiveness and asked him to give his introduction. "I am Hanuman, son of Pawan dev and devotee of Sri Rama" replied Hanuman. I am also your elder brother as you too are the son of Pawan dev. He said that this path is protected by the gods and is cut off to humans. Bheema became happy to meet his elder brother. He requested Hanuman to show his big and distinctive form and Hanuman replied that according to the era, there will be an effect on the body and force and it is impossible for him to take that form in this generation and he showed his form as big as Bheema can see after him insisting again and again. Lord Hanuman's body started gleaming and he seemed like a fire. Now, Bheema started shaking with fear and Hanuman covered his form and became ordinary. He requested Bheema to take a boon from him and Bheema asked him to be with him while conquering his enemies. Hanuman granted him a boon that he will sit in Bheema's flag and roar on the battlefield in such a wild way that the enemies will become scared. He also taught Bheema many skills that he can apply while fighting.

CHAPTER SEVENTEEN

LORD HANUMAN AND SHRI RAM'S DISAPPEARANCE

Maryada Purushottam Sri Rama's death is a mystery. His life was full of suffering. He performed many Yagya's and did social work. Bhu Devi took Sita her daughter away. Later Rama's sons ruled the empire. Sri Rama knew that he has to leave the world as he is born in Mrityuloka and he was waiting for Yama.

One day a saint wanted to meet him in private. This saint was none other than Yama. Yama was afraid to come to Ayodhya as Hanuman was shielding the city. Sri Rama understood what was bothering Yama and he dropped his ring inside a crack of the palace wall and asked Hanuman to get him the ring. Lord Hanuman reduced himself to the size of a beetle and got into the crack. Later he realized that it was an entrance to another world that is Naga Loka, the world of serpents.

Lakshmana also opted to leave his body as Anant Shesha in the Sarayu River. Lord Rama also went into the depth of the Sarayu River and Lord Vishnu appeared to bless Sesh Nag. Hanuman met Vasuki the king of serpents and he even showed Hanuman the ring of Sri Ram. He found an endless number of rings and asked Vasuki about this. Vasuki said that the ring is a representation of the life cycle on the earth. Living beings have to be born and die again and again. Each life cycle is called the 'Kalpa' and each Kalpa has four Yugas. Rama was born in Treta Yuga.

CHAPTER EIGHTEEN

GOSWAMI TULSIDAS

Many books like Ramacharitamanas, Hanuman Chalisa, and Bajrang Baan are written by Goswami Tulsidas. Tulsidas was a saint as well as a poet. He has written many books in Awadhi and Sanskrit. It is believed that he was an incarnation of Valmiki.

According to a few scriptures, Lord Hanuman had gone to the Himalayas, after Rama won the battle over Ravana. There he wrote Ramayana on the rocks with his nails. This version is "Hanuman Nataka". Maharishi Valmiki who met Hanuman there said that this play overshadows the Ramayana written by him. Lord Hanuman was just a devotee of Sri Rama and without wanting any credits he immediately destroyed his writings and asked Valmiki to compose Ramayana in his next birth.

Tulsidas was born in Shukla Paksha, Vikram Samvat, Shravan masa, and Sapthami Tithi. He was born in Uttar Pradesh to Atma Ram Dubey and Hulsi. He was in his mother's womb for twelve months. He had all his teeth during his birth and looked like a five-year-old boy. He did not cry after birth. He was named Rambola by his parents. The astrologers warned his father that this baby will bring danger to his father and his mother Hulsi sent him away with her maid Chuniya. Chuniya passed away when he was five and a half years old and Rambola became an orphan and started begging. It is believed that Goddess Parvathi took care of Rambola in the form of a brahmin woman. Later, Naraharidas adopted him and also performed his thread ceremony at Ayodhya. He took him to Varaha Kshetra Soron. There he listened to Ramayan from a Guru. Later, he learned Sanskrit, astrology, four Vedas, and six Vedangas from Guru Shri Shesha Santana. After all this, he married a beautiful girl named Ratnavali. One day, Tulsidas went to Lord Hanuman's temple and his wife went to her maternal place without informing him and Tulsidas swam across the river Yamuna despite the floods to reach his in-law's place at the night. He didn't want to disturb his in-laws so he climbed a tree and reached his wife's room. Ratnavali said that he is hungry for her body and flesh. She said that even if he had half of such devotion towards God he would have been blessed. Her words hurt him deeply, as he had gone in search of her only because of pure love towards her. He then left to Prayag and renounced his girhasthashram and became a Sadhu. He spent most of his time in Varanasi, Prayag, Ayodhya, and Chitrakoot. He traveled to all the four pilgrimages Dwaraka, Badrinath, Puri, and Rameshwaram. He also visited Manasa Sarovar. He crossed the Ganges. While offering water to a tree, a Phantom appeared and he quenched its thirst. It granted him a boon. Tulsidas asked that he wanted to see Lord Rama. It said that Lord Hanuman will come in the form of a leper to listen to his Ramacharitmanasa and will stay there to listen to it till the end. That day a leper came and sat there till the end. Tulsidas followed this leper and held his feet. The leper tried to ignore him. Tulsidas expressed his desire to see Rama. Lord Hanuman asked him to go to

Chitrakoot.
Tulsidas moved to Chitrakoot and there, he saw two handsome princes but they disappeared immediately. Tulsidas informed everything that happened to Lord Hanuman and he assured him that he will get a chance to see Sri Rama once again.

One day, two handsome children came to Tulsidas and asked for sandalwood. Tulsidas became hypnotized by these two princes' looks. Rama himself took the sandalwood and applied it on his forehead and even on Tulsidas's forehead before disappearing.

Tulsidas composed Ramacharitamanas in Awadhi according to Lord Shiva's instructions. He became popular because of the vernacular language he used to write his poetry. Due to god's grace on him, he created many works such as Dohavali, Geetavali, Karitavali, and Vinaya Patrika and sacrificed his body.

CHAPTER NINETEEN

BERMUDA TRIANGLE MYSTERY

We all know 'Bermuda Triangle' for its mystery. It is located in the western part of the North Atlantic Ocean. Many ships and aircraft have vanished from this region. This place has invisible forces that attract ships, vessels, and aircraft. It is also known as 'Devil's triangle' or 'Hurricane alley.

When Lord Hanuman was crossing the ocean in search of Sita a demoness named 'Simhika' attracted him to her. The demoness was also known as 'Chayagrahi'. She had received a boon from Lord Brahma that she could attract all living beings passing through the sea. Lord Hanuman had observed that this demoness is pulling him towards her using his shadow and was trying to eat him. Lord Hanuman made his body big and tall till he reached the sky. Simhika opened her mouth wide and immediately, Lord Hanuman reduced himself and became a tiny form. He entered inside her and ripped her inner organs and came out by her breasts. It is believed that after slaying Ravana, Rama gave the gem which was released from Ravana's navel to Lord Hanuman and asked him to preserve it carefully. Lord

Hanuman then hid the gem inside this deep ocean.

CHAPTER TWENTY

SANKAT MOCHAN HANUMAN ASTAK

Baal samai ravi bhakshi liyo tab, teenahu loka bhayo andhiyaro
Taahi so traas bhayo jag ko, yah sankat kaahu so jaat na taro
Dewan aani kari bintee tab, chaadhi diyo ravi kast niwaaro
Ko nahi jaanat hai jag mei kapi sankat mochan ram tihaaro

During your childhood, you attempted to swallow the sun
And the world filled with sorrow, you were the only hope to them
You recovered from the disease afflicted by the sun
You remove ignorance by knowledge and who doesn't know your name in this world?

Baali ki traas kapees basai giri, jaat mahaprabhu panth niharo
Chownki maha muni saap diyo tab chahiy kaun bichaar bichaaro
Kai dwij roop liwaay maha prabhu so tum daas ke sok niwaaro
Ko nahi jaanat hai jag mei kapi sankat mochan naam tiharo

You protected Sugriva from Vali, by asking him to live in a mountain

Where Bali was not allowed to enter as he was cursed by "Chauki saint"
You disguised as a brahmin and met Shri Ram and you killed Bali
Thus you relieved a devotee from his sorrow
Who in this world does not know that your name is SANKAT MOCHA HANUMAN
The remover of ignorance by your knowledge

Angad ke sang laiye gaye siya, khoj kapees yah baain uchaaro,
jeevat na bachihau hum son ju, bina sudhi laay ehaan pagu dhaaro
Hayri thake tatt sindhu sabaai tab laay siya-sudhi praan ubaro
Ko nahi janat hai jag me kapi sankat mochan naam tiharo

You went to Angad to get information about Sita,
At the sea-coast Angad told "We will not remain alive if we fetched information about Sita"
All became tired but you went to collect information about Sita and saved the entire troop
Who in this world, does not know your name and that you are Sankat mochan?

Raavan traas dayee siya ko sab, raakshasi so kahi sok nivaro
Taahi samay hanuman Mahaprabhu, Jaay mahaa rajneechar maaro
Chaahat seeya asok so aagi su, dai prabhu mudrika sok nivaro
Ko nahin janat hai jag mei kapi sankat mochan raam tiharo

When Ravana was torturing Sita by instructing the maids to harass her,
You reached there and killed many enemies
When Sita was out of trouble she asked for fire from the

Ashoka tree
And you gave Sri Ram's ring to her and delivered his message to her
In this way, you gave hope to Sita
So who does not know you as Sankat mochan Hanuman in this world?

Baan lagyo ur Lakshyman ke tab, praan taje sut raavan maro
Lai griha baidya sushen samet, tabai grini dron su beer upaaro
Aani sanjeevan hath dayee taba lakshiman ke tum praan upaaro
Ko nahin janat hai jag me kapi sankat mochan naam tiharo

When an arrow struck Lakshman's heart,
You brought 'Sushen Vaidya' who asked you to get 'Sanjeevani herb'
And you brought the entire Dron mountain and saved Lakshmana
Who in this world does not know your name is Sankat Mochan Hanuman?

Raavan yudh ajaan kiyo tab, naag ki phaas sabhi sir daro
Shri Raghunath samet sabai dal, moh bhayo yah sankat bhaaro
aani khagesh tabai Hanumaan ju, bandhan kaati sutraas nivaro
Ko nahi janat hai jag mei kapi sankat mochan naam tiharo

When Ravan attacked Shri Rama's army by tying snakes around them while they were sleeping,
The whole army including Rama was in trouble
Then you bought Gaduda, the big eagle to help them
And you saved Sri Rama's army
Who in this world does not know your name as Sankat Mochan Hanuman?

Bandhu samet jabai ahiraavan, lai raghunath pataal sidharo
Devhi puji bhalee vidhi so bali, deu sabai mili mantra vicharo
Jay sahaay bhayo tab hi ahiravan sainya samet sanharo
Ko nahi janat hai jag me kapi sankat mochan naam tiharo

When Ahiravan kidnapped, Shri Ram and Lakshman to patal
When they were about to give human sacrifice,
You appeared there and killed Ahiravan
Who does not know your name as Sankat Mochan?

Kaaj Kiye barh dewan kei tum, beer mahaaprabhu dekhi bicaro
Kaun sa sankat mohin gareeb ko, jo tumson nahi jaat hai taro
Begi haro Hanuman mahaprabhu jo kuch sankat hoya humharo
Ko nahi jaanat hai jag me kapi sankat mochan naam tiharo

You have done great work for Shri Ram and many other gods,
Tell me which obstacles are not removed by your glimpse,
Oh, Hanuman! Please remove obstacles from my life as you are my guru,
Who in this world does not know you Sankat Mochan Hanuman?

Doha
Laal deh laalee lase, aru dhari laal langoor
Bajra deh danavadalan, jai jai jai kapi soor

You have a red body that is giving light to the whole world,
You spied Lanka in disguise, Your body is like a thunderbolt and can kill enemy
You enlighten the gods, and I meditate upon you.

CHAPTER TWENTY-ONE

HANUMAN CHALISA

"Shree Guru Charan Saroj Raj
Nij Manu Mukur Sudhari
Baranau Raghuvar Vimal Jasu
Jo Daayaku Phal Chaari"
After cleaning my mind with the guru's Lotus feet dust, I profess the glory of Shri Ram, who gives the four-fold fruits of life (ie. Dharma, Artha, Kama, and Moksha).
"Buddhi-hin-Tanujaanike, Sumirau Pawan Kumar,
Bal Buddhi Vidya Dehu Mohi, Harahu Kalesh Vikar"
I am aware of my lack of intelligence, so Oh son of the Air, I urge you to bestow me strength, intelligence, wisdom to remove all my flaws.
Jai Hanuman Gyaan Gun Sagar
Jay Kapis Tihun Lok Ujaagar
O Hanuman, Ocean of wisdom and virtue, the Lord of monkeys, light up the three worlds with your glory.
"Ram Doot Atulit Bal Dhama
Anjani-Putra Pawansut Namaa"
You are the divine messenger of Lord Shri Rama and son of mother Anjani and wind.
"Mahaavir Bikram Bajrangi
Kumati Niwaar Sumati Ke Sangi"

Oh Hanuman, you are brave. You are the dispeller of darkness and companion of good sense.

"Kanchan Baran Biraaj Subesa
Kaanan Kundal Kunchit Kesa"

Your build is handsome and is golden in color and your dress is pretty. You have curly hair and you wear earrings.

"Haath Bajra Auo Dwaja Biraaje
Khaande Munj Janeu Saaje"

Your hands are like thunderbolts and you carry a Kesari color flag in one hand and a cudgel in another hand. You wear a thread across his shoulder.

"Shankar Suvan Keshri Nanadan
Tej Prataap Maha Jag Vandan"

You have originated from Lord Shiva and you are the son of Keshari. You are full of luster and are lovable of all.

"Vidyavaan Guni Ati Chaatur
Ram Kaaj Karibe Ko Atur"

You are wise and skillful. You are eager to do the work of Shri Ram.

"Prabhu Charit Sunibe ko Rasiya
Ram Lakhan Sita Man Basiya"

You are always eager to listen to Lord Ram's life stories. Ram, Lakshman, and Sita dwell in your heart.

"Sookshm Roop Dhari Siyahi Dikhawa
Bikat Roop Dhari Lanka Jaraava"

You appeared in front of Sita in a very tiny form
In your powerful form, you burnt Lanka.

"Bhim Roop Dhari Asur Sanhare
Ramchandra Ke Kaaj Saware"

You killed demons in Lanka and handled all responsibilities of Sri Ram with skill.

"Laay Sanjeevan Lakhan Jiyaye
Shree Raghubir Harashi Ur Laye"

You brought the " Sanjeevani" herb and made Lakshman alive and Lord Ram hugged you with a heart full of love.

"Raghupati Kinhi Bahut Badai
Tum Mam Priye Bharatahi Sam Bhai"

Sri Rama praised you a lot for this act of yours and said that 'you are like my brother "Bharatha"'.

"Sahastra Badan Tumharo Jas Gaave
Asa Kahi Shripati Kanth Lagaave"

Thousands of living beings are singing hymns of your glories
Saying this Lord Rama hugged you.

"Sankaadik Brahmadi Munisa
Naarad Saarad Sahit Ahisa"

Not only Lord Rama but Lord Brahma, the great sage Narada, and goddess Saraswathi along with the snake Ahisa, praise your glories.

"Jam Kuber Digpaal Jahaan Te
Kabin Kobid Kahi Sake Kahaan Te"

Even the god of death, the god of wealth, and the Digpaal who are protecting the four corners of this universe praise your glories.

"Tum Upkaar Sugrivahin Keenha
Ram Milay Raaj Pad Deenha"

You did a big favor to Sugriva and introduced him to Lord Ram and he got the Royal throne because of you.

"Tumharo mantra Bibhishan Maana
Lankeshwar Bhay Sab Jag Jaana"

Vibhishan supported Lord Rama and he announced you as the king of Lanka. This is known to all.

"Jug Sahastra Jojan Par Bhanu
Lilyo Tahi Madhur Fal Janu"

You swallowed the huge sun which is at a distance of many million kilometers away from the earth thinking that it is an

appetizing fruit.
Prabhu Mudrika Meli Mukh Maahin
Jaladhi Langhi Gaye Achraj Naahin"
You carried Sri Ram's ring in your mouth and leaped into the sea immediately.
"Durgam Kaaj Jagat Ke Jete
Sugam Anugrah Tumhare Tete"
All difficult things become easy to perform by your grace.
"Ram Duaare Tum Rakhvare
Hoat Na Aagya Binu Paisare"
You guard Shri Ram's door and no one can enter it without your consent.
Sab Sukh Lahai Tumhari Sarna
Tum Rakshak Kaahu Ko Darana"
All comfort of the world lies at your feet and the devotees feel protected in your shelter.
"Aapan Thej Sambharo Aape
Tino Lok Haank Ten Kaanpe"
When you roar, you can control your huge energy, and the three worlds, tremor.
"Bhut Pisaach Nikat Nahin Aaveh
Mahabir Jab Naam Sunaavai"
All the evil energies never come near when they hear your name.
"Naasai Rog Hare Sab Peera
Japat Nirantar Hanumat Beera"
All diseases and body pain disappear by reciting your name.
"Sankat Te Hanuman Chhudaave
Man Kram Bachan Dhyan Jo Laavai"
You will save all odds in the life of those who remember you genuinely.
"Sab Par Ram Tapasvi Raaja

Tin Ke Kaaj Sakal Tum Saaja"
You help all those who have faith in Shri Ram as if it is your responsibility.
"Aur Manorath Jo Koi Lavaai
Soi Amit Jeevan Phal Pavai"
Whoever comes to you for the fulfillment of any desire with sincerity and faith, will get the nectar fruit of life.
"Charo Jug Partap Tumhaara
Hai Parsiddha Jagat Ujiyara"
Your glory is praised in all four eras. Your fame is noted all over the Universe.
"Saadhu Sant Ke Tum Rakhvare
Asur Nikandhan Ram Dulaare"
You are the savior of Saints and the favorite of Shri Raam.
"Asht Siddhi Nau Nidhi Ke Daata
Ash Bar Deen Jaanaki Maata"
You went to Lanka to meet Sita and she blessed you that you can grant the eight Siddis to anyone and nine Nidhis like riches, comfort, fame, power, etc.
"Ram Rasayan Tumhare Pasa
Sada Raho Raghupati Ke Daasa"
You hold the blessings of Rama and are a follower of him.
"Tumhare Bhajan Ram Ko Paavai
Janam Janam Ke Dukh Bisraavai"
Your devotee can get the forgiveness of Rama and become free from the distress of several births and can attain Moksha.
"Anta Kaal Raghubar Pur Jaai
Jahaan Janm Haribhakt Kahaai"
If one during death, goes to Rama, he will attain Moksha.
"Aur Devata Chitt Na Dharai
Hanumat Seyi Sarv Sukh Karayi"
If you are a devotee of Hanuman then there is no need to

worship any other god as he is capable of fulfilling all your desires.

"Sankat Katai Mite Sab Pira
Jo Sumirai Hanumat Balbira"

If you remember Lord Hanuman you will be free from all miseries, sufferings, and the cycle of rebirth.

"Jo Sath Baar Paat Kar Koi
Chutahi Bandi Maha Sukh Hoyi"

If a person recites Hanuman Chalisa, hundred times regularly, he becomes free from the bondage of life and death.

"Jo Yeh Padhai Hanuman Chalisa
Hoy Siddhi Saaki Gaurisa"

All those who recite Hanuman Chalisa regularly will become successful in everything. This is witnessed by Lord Shiva.

"Tulsidaas Sada Hari Chera
Keejay Naath Hridaya Maha Dera"

Tulsidas as a bonded devotee of Lord Hanuman prays" Oh Lord, please reside in my heart forever",

"Pawan Tanay Sankat Haran
Mangal Murati Roop"

"O Conquerer of wind, O destroyer of all miseries, you are a symbol of auspiciousness.

"Ram Lakhan Sita Sahit
Hridaya Basahu Sur Bhup"

"O Hanuman, please reside in my heart along with Ram, Laxman, and Sita forever".

9 798886 847536

Printed by Libri Plureos GmbH in Hamburg,
Germany